I0472326

Cheltenham and Terra Cotta Ontario in Colour Photos, Saving Our History One Photo at a Time

Photography
by Barbara Raué
©2019

Series Name: Cruising Ontario

Book 235: Cheltenham, Terra Cotta

Cover photo: 14376 Creditview Road, Cheltenham, Page 5

Series Name: Cruising Ontario
Saving Our History One Photo at a Time
in colour photos

Books Available in Alphabetical Order:
Aberfoyle, Acton, Ajax, Alton, Amherstburg, Ancaster, Arthur, Auburn, Aylmer, Ayr, Beaver Valley, Belgrave, Belleville, Bloomingdale, Blyth, Brantford, Brockville, Burford, Burlington, Caledon, Caledonia, Cambridge, Carlow, Chatsworth, Clifford, Collingwood, Conestogo, Delhi, Dorchester to Aylmer, Drayton, Drumbo, Dundas, Dunlop, Eden Mills, Elmira, Elora, Erin, Essex, Fergus, Goderich, Grimsby, Guelph, Hagersville, Hamilton, Hanover, Harriston, Hespeler, Jarvis, Kingston, Kingsville, Kitchener, Lake Superior, Lincoln, Linwood, Listowel, London, Lucknow, Merrickville, Mono, Mount Forest, Mount Pleasant, Neustadt, New Hamburg, Newboro, Newport, Niagara-on-the-Lake, Niagara Falls, North Bay, Oakville, Onondaga, Orangeville, Orillia, Oshawa, Owen Sound, Palmerston, Paris, Pelham, Perth, Peterborough, Petrolia, Pickering, Port Colborne, Port Elgin, Portland, Preston, Rockwood, Sarnia, Sault Ste. Marie, Seaforth, Sheffield, Shelburne, Simcoe, Smiths Falls, Smithville, Southampton, St. Catharines, St. George, St. Jacobs, St. Marys, St. Thomas, Stoney Creek, Stratford, Thamesford, Thunder Bay, Tillsonburg, Toronto, Waterdown, Waterford, Waterloo, Welland, Wellesley, West Flamborough, Westport, Whitby, Windsor, Wingham, Woodstock

Book 218-219: Uxbridge
Book 220: Port Perry
Book 221-222: Stouffville
Book 223: Colborne
Book 224: Grafton, Bolton
Book 225-229: Cobourg

Book 230-233: Port Hope
Book 234: Belfountain
Book 235:Cheltenham,TerraCotta

Table of Contents

Cheltenham   Page 5

Terra Cotta   Page 27

Boston Mills Road   Page 40

Cheltenham - In 1816 Charles and Martha Haines and three children left England for New York; the following year they arrived in York, Upper Canada, where Charles, a millwright, built mills. In 1819, the Chinguacousy Township survey was completed and Haines purchased 100 acres along the Credit River with a mill site west of Creditview Road. The Haines family settled in what he named 'Cheltenham' after his birthplace. It is located north-west of Brampton.

In 1827 he built a grist mill, dammed the river and chiseled mill stones. In 1842, Frederick Haines, the second son, built Cheltenham's first store. In 1845, the first tavern was built and run by C. Spence. In 1847, to meet demand, Haines built a larger mill with three runs of stone, and he constructed a saw mill on the south side of the river. In 1848, William Henry built an Inn. In 1850,the first blacksmith shop was built. In 1852, Cheltenham post office opened with William Allan as first postmaster. By 1853, Cheltenham had three hotels.

In the 1860s, the commercial core expanded with the addition of four shoe stores, a saddlery, and two cabinet makers. In 1874, the Hamilton & Northwestern Railway arrived north of the village (later became CNR). In 1877, the Credit Valley Railway arrived about one kilometer east of the village, accessed by Station Road. In the 1870s, Kee's steam tannery was started and two distilleries produced 'Cheltenham Wheat Whisky'. In 1887, fire destroyed a major block of buildings; rebuilding began. In 1914, Interprovincial Brick Company opened a plant just west of the village center.

In 1822, Joseph Kenny was awarded a Crown Grant in Chinguacousy Township of 100 acres along the Credit River on which much of Terra Cotta now sits. It is located south of Cheltenham. In 1857, Henry Tucker purchased 40 acres from Kenny to build grist and saw mills powered by a dam and mill race on the Credit River. Simon Plewes bought the mills in 1859 and the hamlet became known as Plewes Mills.

By the time a church, the Wesleyan Methodist Church, was built in 1862 the village had been renamed Salmonville for the annual spawning frenzy. A post office opened in 1866 and by 1874 there were thirty-four surveyed lots in the hamlet on the banks of the Credit River.

This early community spread westwards and straddled the boundary of Chinguacousy and Esquesing townships. This divided the village schoolchildren, their two schoolhouses being in opposite directions. By 1873 the village had acquired telegraph facilities, two sawmills and a grist mill, and in 1877 the Hamilton & Northwestern Railway arrived, stimulating local industry and farm exports.

Industry began with brickworks exploiting the local red clay, and by 1891 the post office was renamed Terra Cotta. In the 1930s, the brickworks became victims of the Depression and only a kiln chimney remains. Quarries east of Terra Cotta were established in the 1840s and the arrival of the railway broadened their market reach, allowing local sandstone to be used as far away as Ottawa in the Parliament Buildings.

In the 1940s, community enterprise expanded into recreation. The river's abundant water resources were used to develop Clancy's Ranch as a weekend resort, expanded in 1949 into Terra Cotta Playground, and purchased in 1958 by Credit Valley Conservation.

Cheltenham

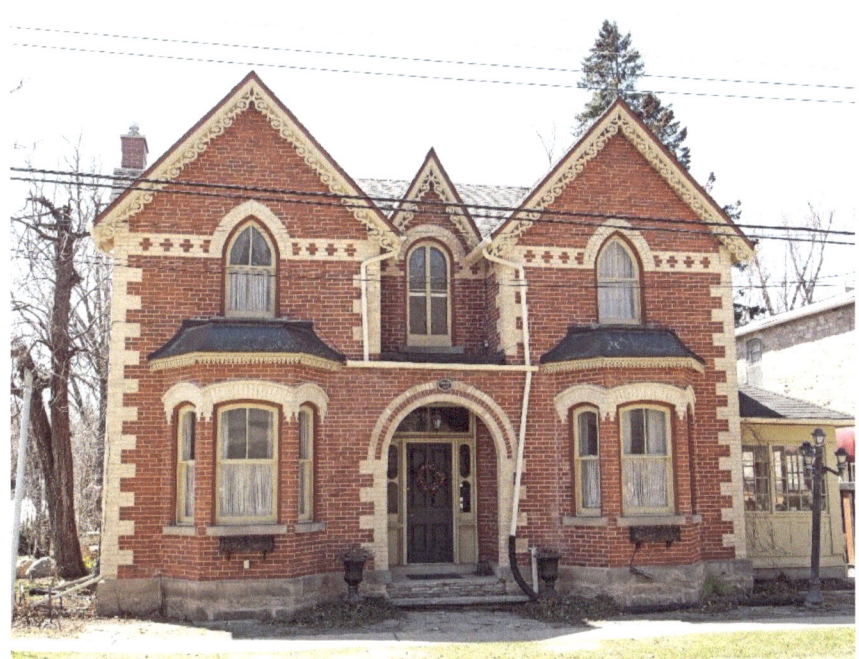

14376 Creditview Road - Frederick Haines House - circa 1887 - After losing his first home to the 1887 fire, entrepreneur Frederick Haines, son of Cheltenham's founder, built this red brick house with intricate yellow brick patterning. Later additions are compatible with the original three gable Victorian Gothic style. In the 1940s-1950s, it became a United Church rest and holiday home. It later housed an antique shop before being converted back to a private residence. It has a bell cast roof over each front bay, an arched entry and etched glass transom and sidelights of the central entrance.

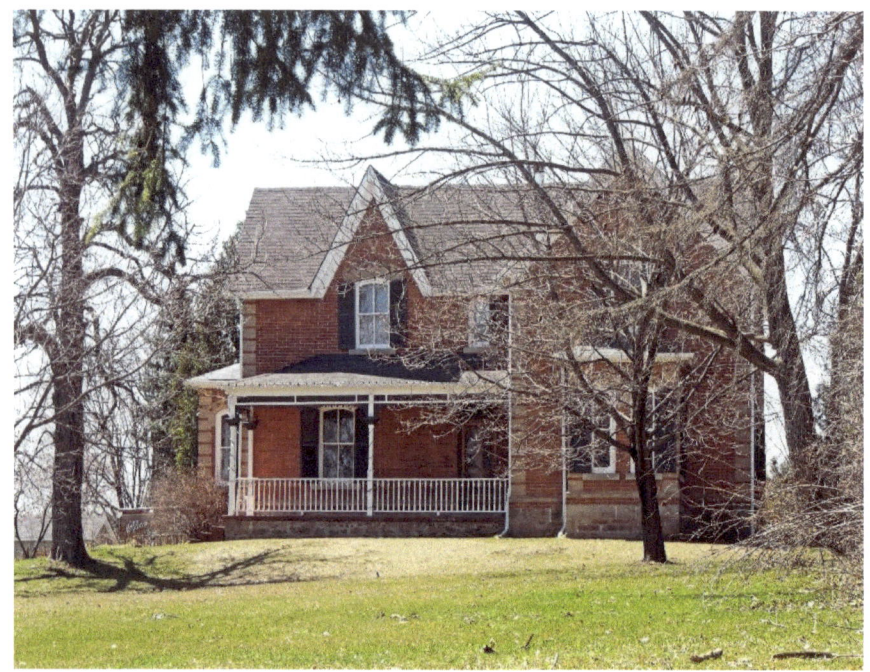

14700 Creditview Road - Joseph Little House - 1861 or earlier - Originally a single storey cottage on a fieldstone foundation, this 1½ storey frame house was built for English farmer Joseph Little and his wife Jane. It grew and evolved into a Victorian Gothic style house with a classic centre gable. A red brick veneer with yellow brick patterning was applied over the original, probably stucco, exterior cladding. In 1877, Little sold a parcel of land to the Hamilton & Northwestern Railway for its Cheltenham station.

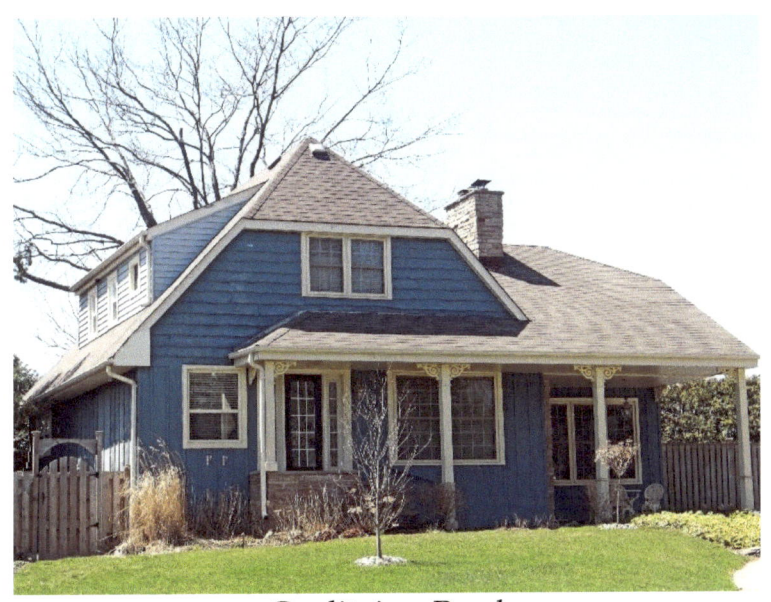

Creditview Road

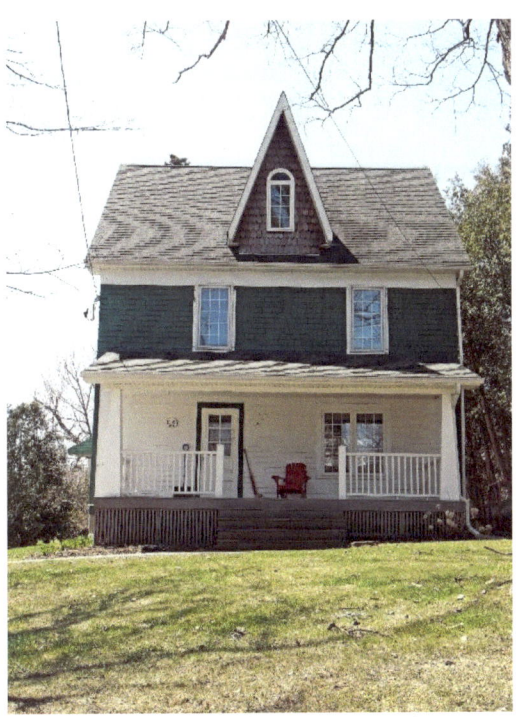

14596 Creditview Road

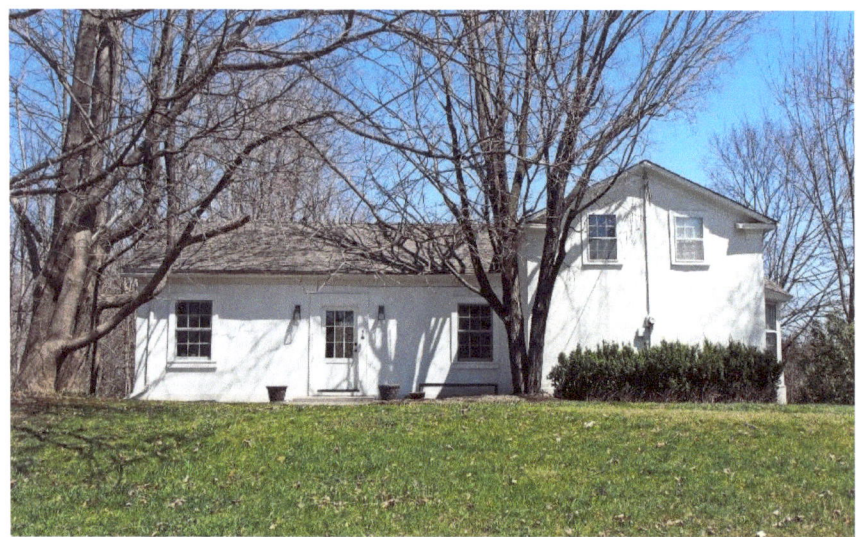

14529 Creditview Road - Farm House - mid-1850s - This rectangular frame house was probably built by Samuel Snell on land severed from the original 100-acre farm. Later owners included Samuel and Mary Ann Brown. It faces south instead of west to the street, an orientation which provided greater access to sunlight in winter months. Its shallow gable roof, returned eaves and lack of decorative trim are Neo-Classical in style, while the projecting bay window with its original cedar shingle roof and stucco exterior is more typical of early Victorian style.

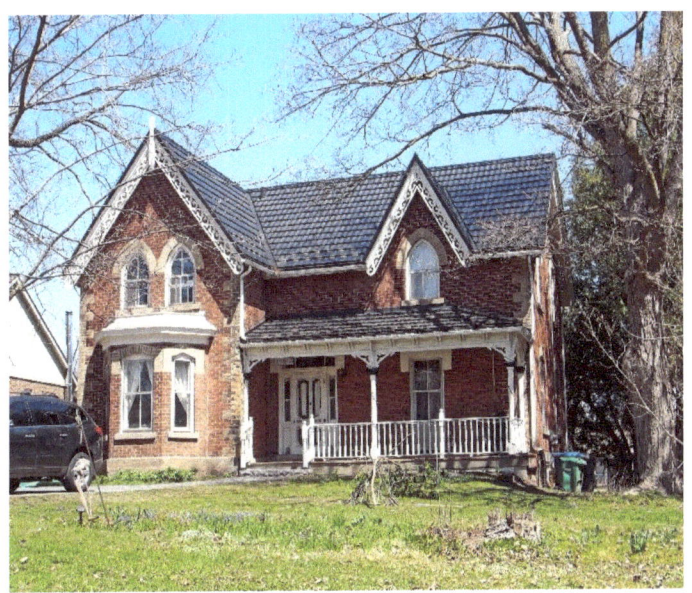

14515 Creditview Road

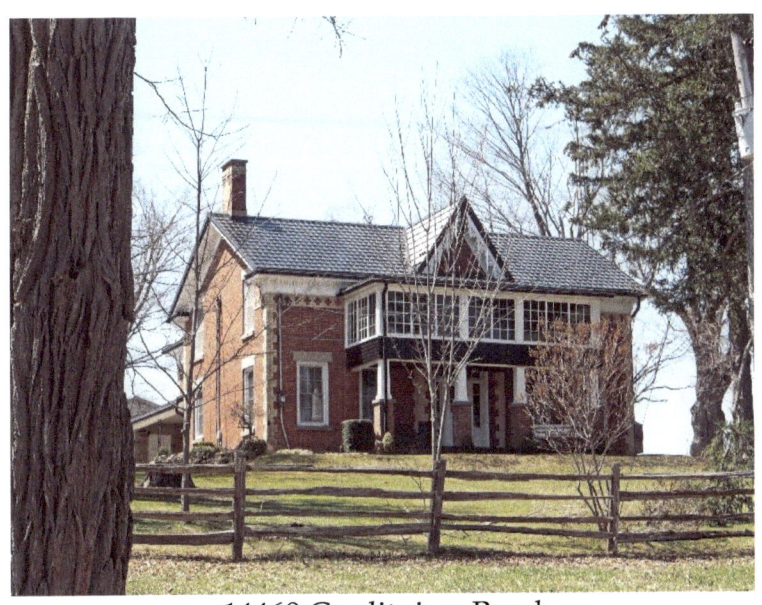

14460 Creditview Road

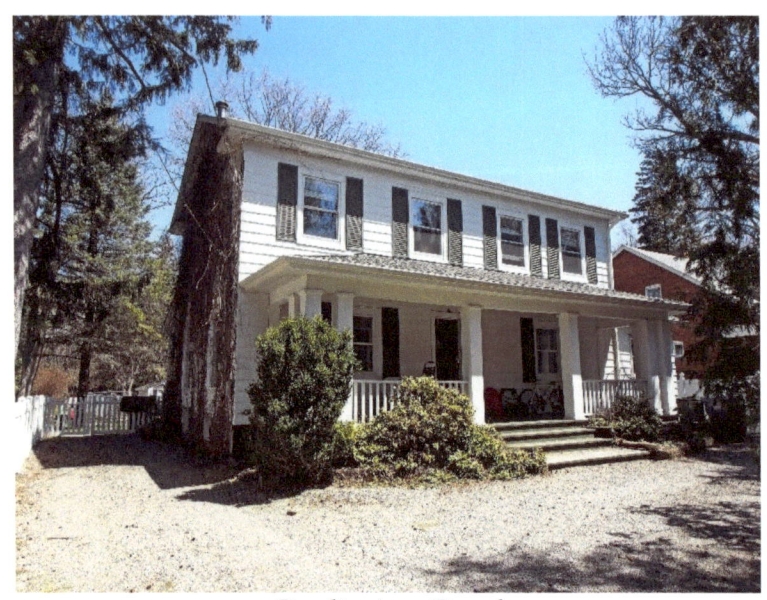

Creditview Road

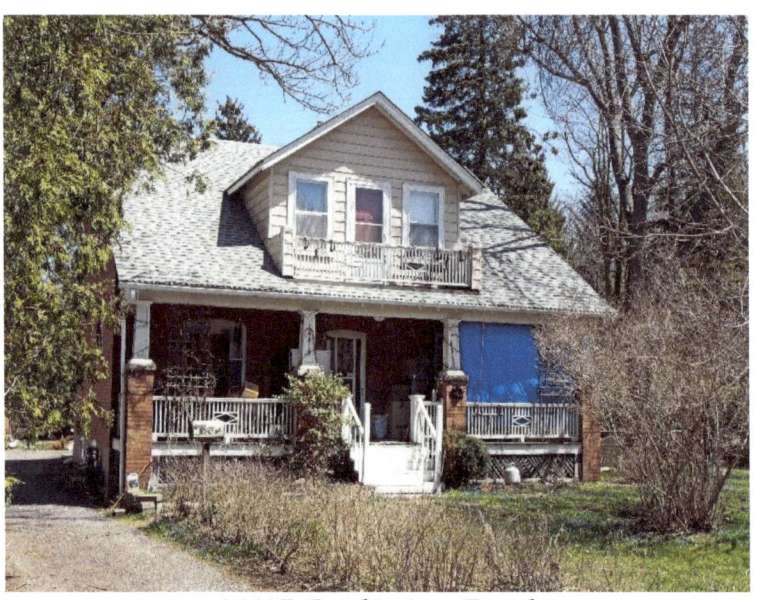

14415 Creditview Road

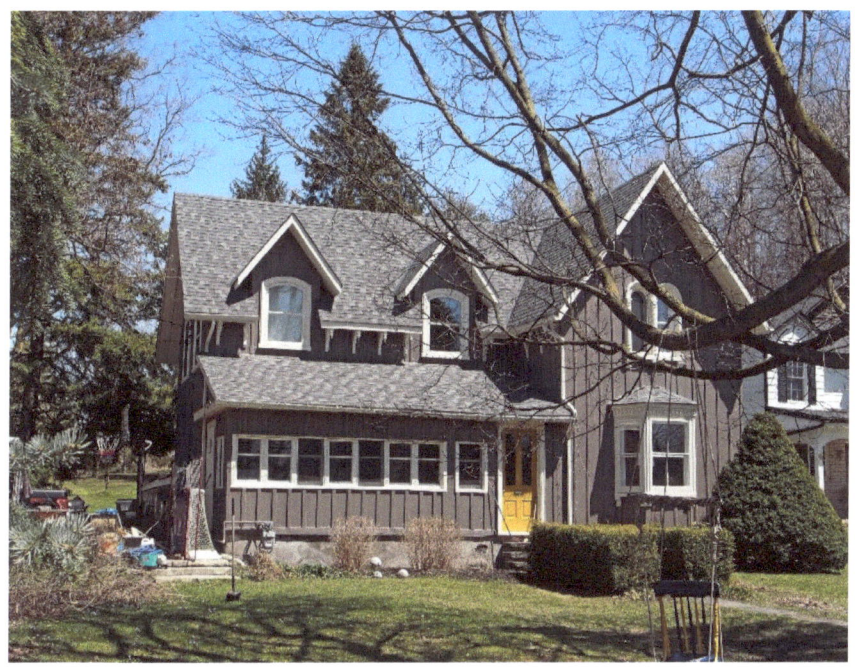

14411 Creditview Road - King Store/Residence - circa 1870s - This Victorian Gothic general store/residence was built for Charles King, a Cheltenham merchant. In the 1880s, it became the Harris General Store with John and MaryAnn Harris living in the residence. Postmaster Albert Kee purchased it in 1928, removed the store portion and ran the post office here until 1931. His widow, Ada Louise Kee, took over as postmistress until she retired in 1958. There are cornice brackets on the eaves and there is a double Gothic window above the front bay window.

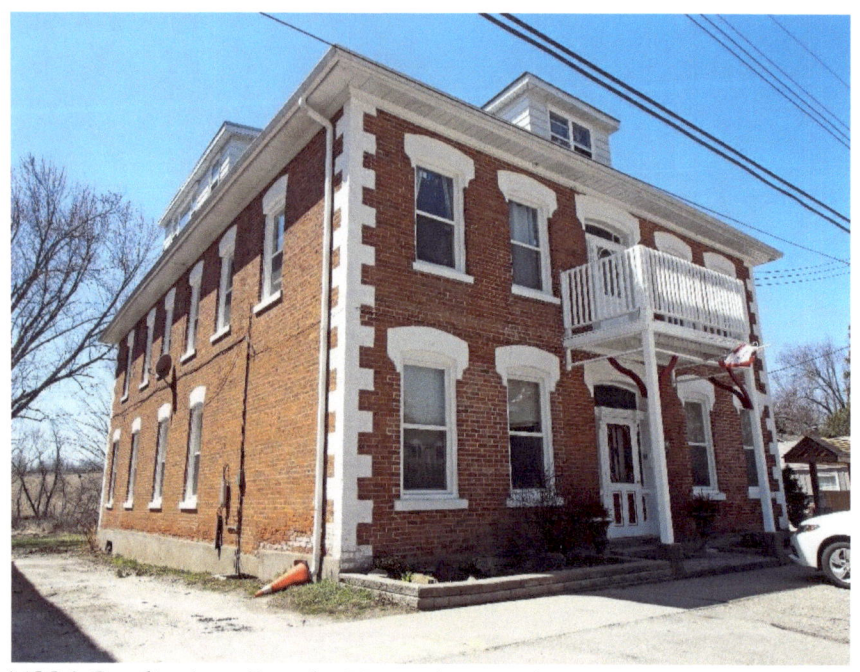

14396 Creditview Road - Henry's Hotel - circa 1887 - William Henry's pre-1859 Inn was destroyed in the 1887 fire. He rebuilt, replacing the Inn with this two-storey Georgian style frame building with hip roof and brick veneer. He named it 'Henry's Hotel' operating it until his death in 1904. Thomas and Nathaniel Browne took it over as 'Browne's Hotel'. It was later a butcher shop with home above. In 1958 it was adapted to commercial/apartment use.

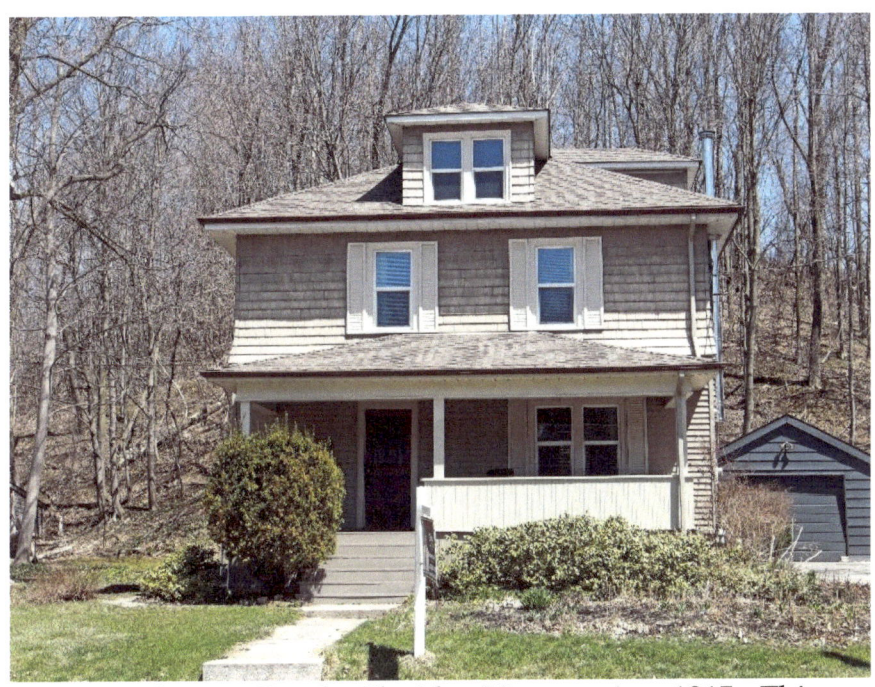

14387 Creditview Road - Claridge House - circa 1915 - This 'four-square' frame house is built in the Edwardian Classical style characterized by an asymmetrical floor plan, pyramidal hipped roof and large attic dormers. The partially enclosed verandah has a roof slope that matches that of house roof above. The original owner was a carpenter.

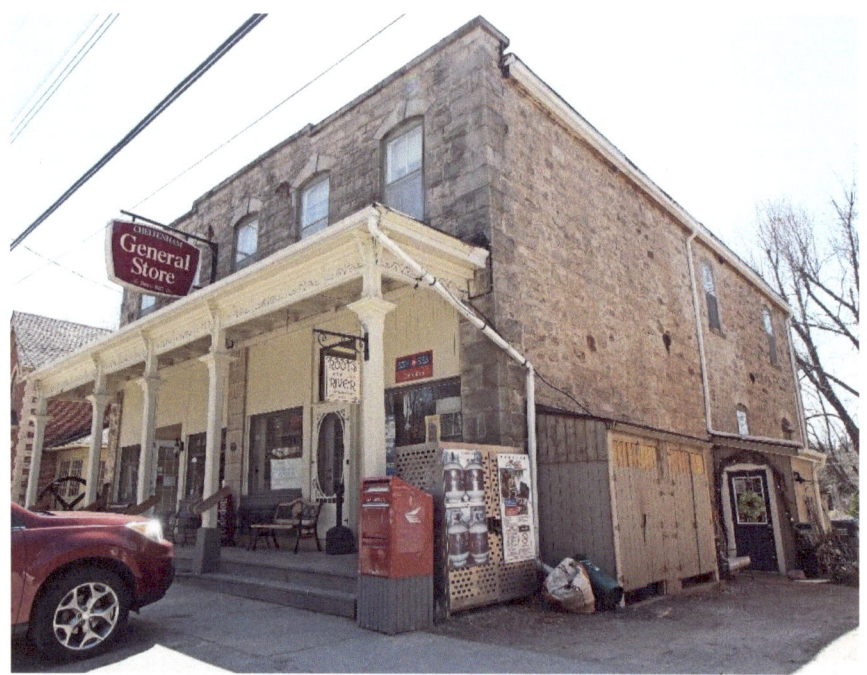

14386 Creditview Road - Cheltenham General Store - circa 1887 - This large square limestone and sandstone structure was built by Frederick Haines after the 1887 fire destroyed its frame predecessor. It is Caledon's only stone general store. There are projecting keystones on the curved window tops, and the classic storefront windows are shaded by a wooden, flat-roofed verandah with decorative posts.

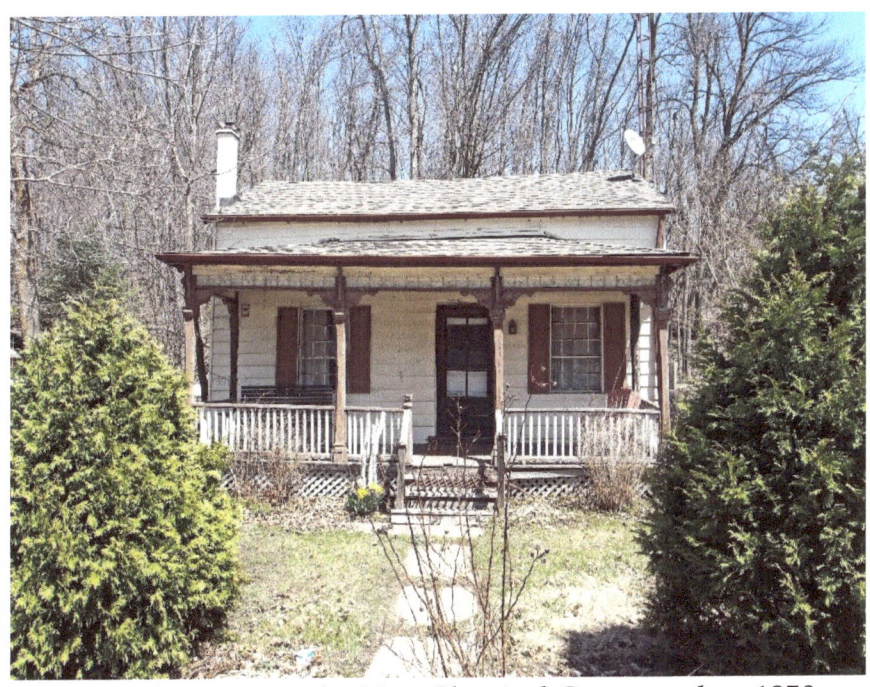

14377 Creditview Road – Neo-Classical Cottage - late 1850s - This 1½ storey frame cottage was likely built by John Lyons. It was sold soon after to Thomas Mercer who lived here for the next 20 years. The covered verandah with its hip roof has a banister running from both sides to the central entrance/steps along with a decorative frieze under the eaves.

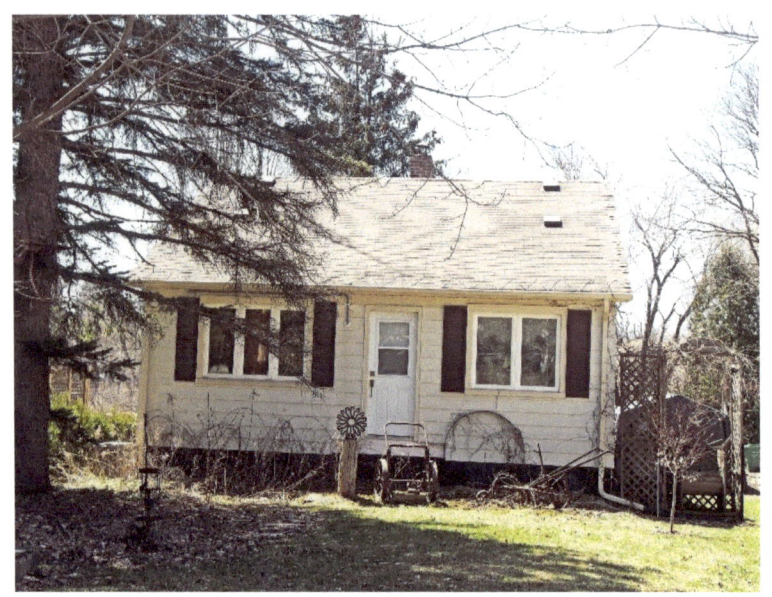

Creditview Road

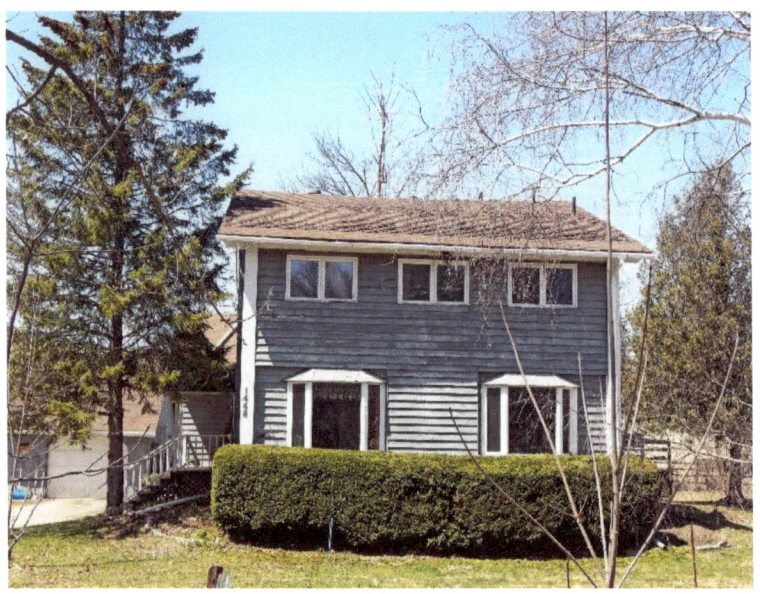

1448 Mill Street

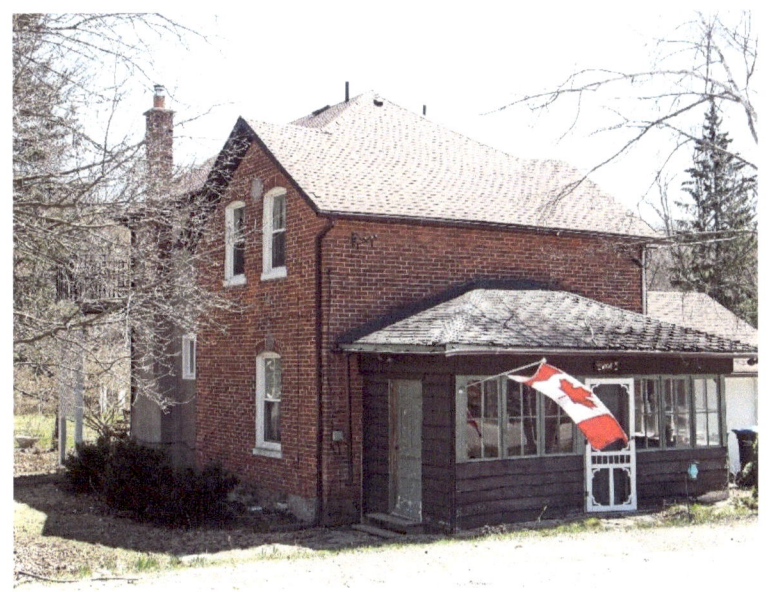

Mill Street

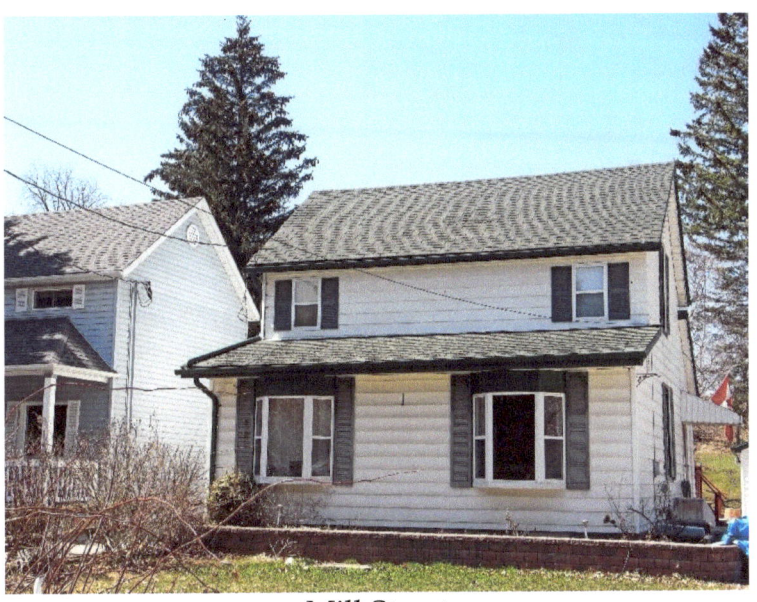

Mill Street

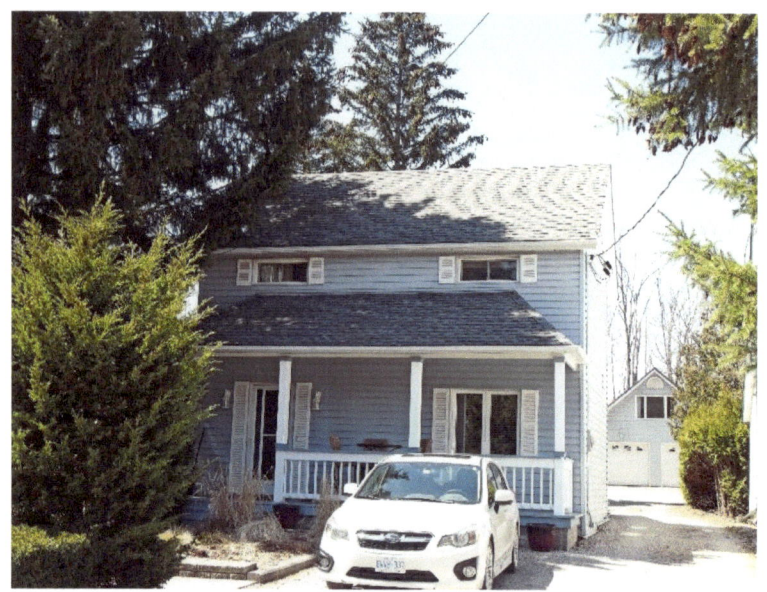

Mill Street

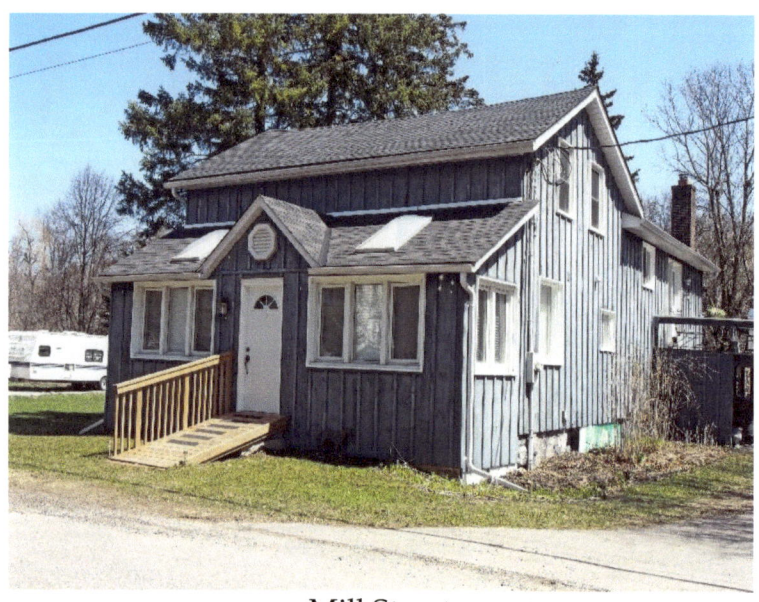

Mill Street

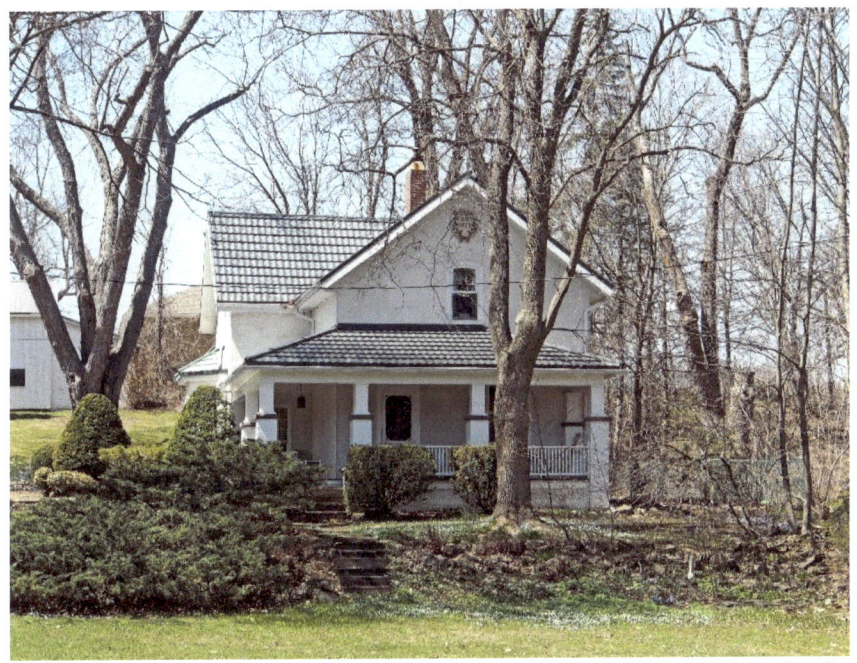

1406 Mill Street - Haines-Reid House - circa 1877 - Typical of late 19th century urban architecture, this 1½ storey Victorian Gothic frame home was built for Charles Haines, a nephew of Cheltenham's founder. Its stucco exterior is original, as is the date plaque set into the front-end gable. Set well back from the road on a rise, the property's mature trees contribute to its historic streetscape context.

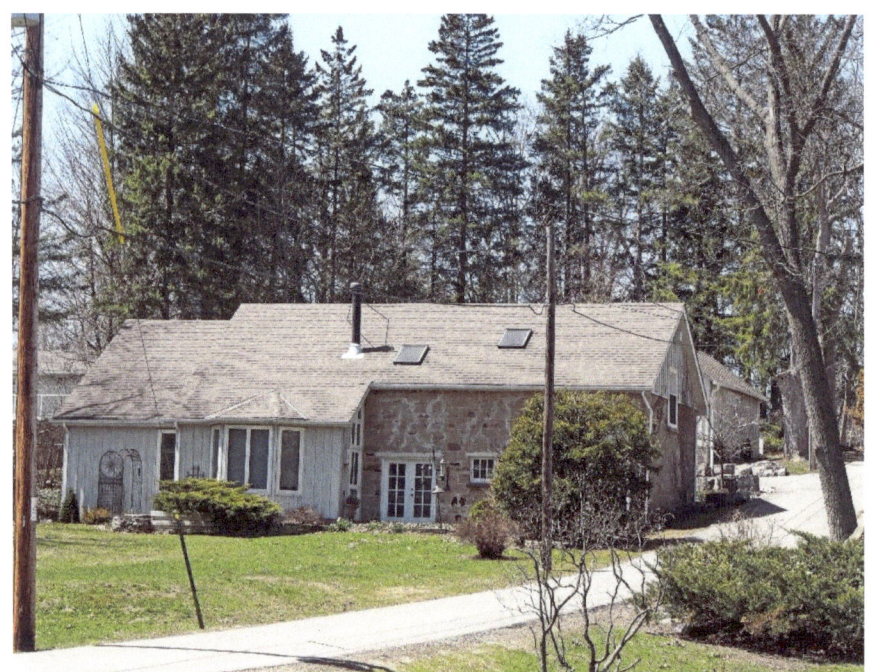

1402 Mill Street - Small Stone Barn - circa 1890 - This unique dwelling incorporates a small stone barn originally built as an outbuilding on property owned by the Haines family. In 1956, the barn was converted to residential use and the owners skillfully retained its physical integrity along with the original door and window openings. The current owner purchased it in 1994 and completed the more recent frame additions.

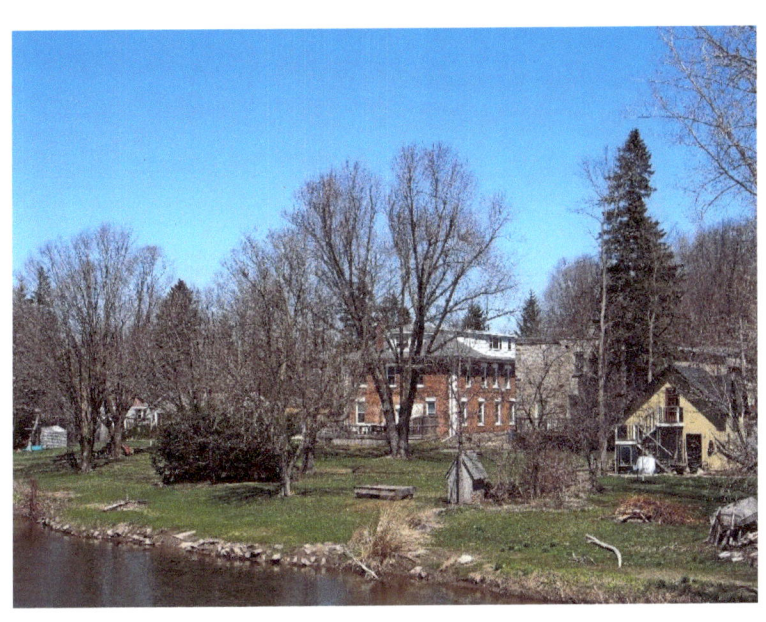

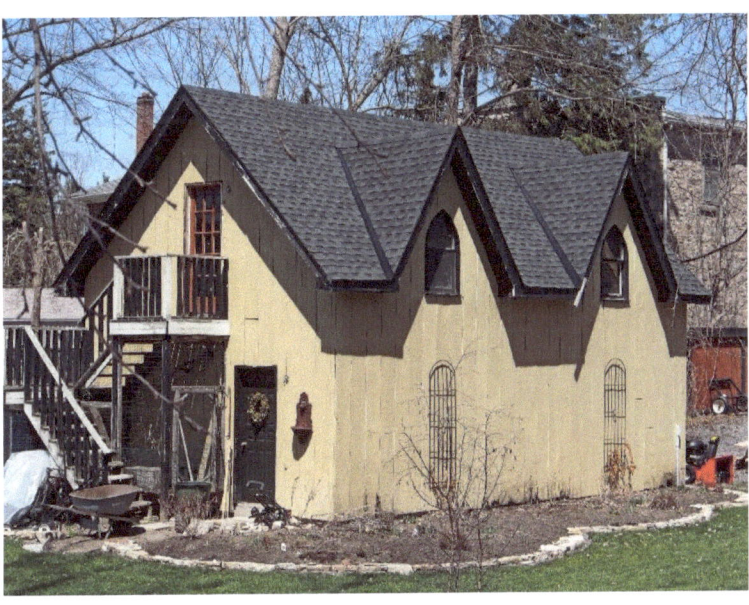

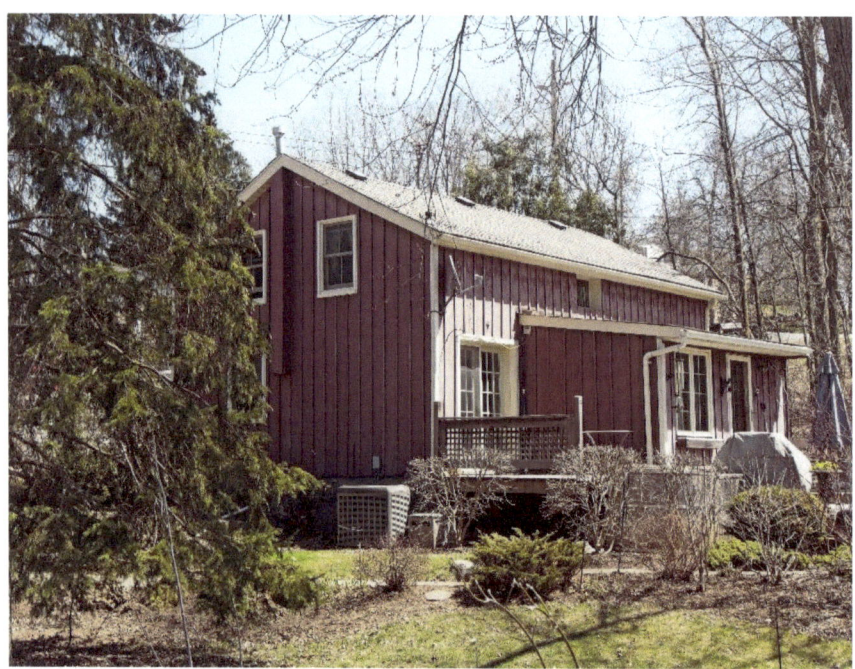

1499 Mill Street - Horatio Haines Cottage - circa 1847-1851 - This 1½ storey, timber frame Georgian style cottage is unique with its identical front and rear facades, providing views to the grist and saw mills across the river and to the developing village core. Haines family members were its builders, carpenters, lumber suppliers and intended occupants, the first being Horatio Haines, miller and fifth son of Charles and Martha Haines. Horatio died in 1856, aged 32 and it was later sold to his brother Frederick.

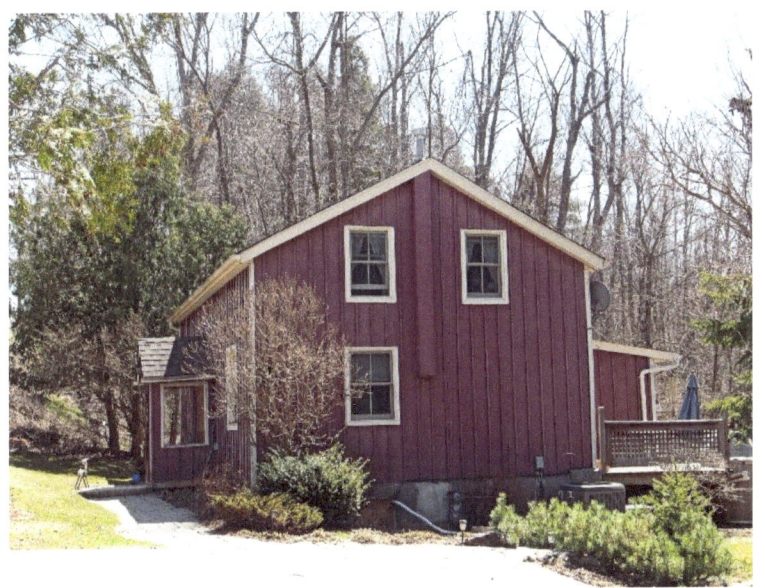

1499 Mill Street

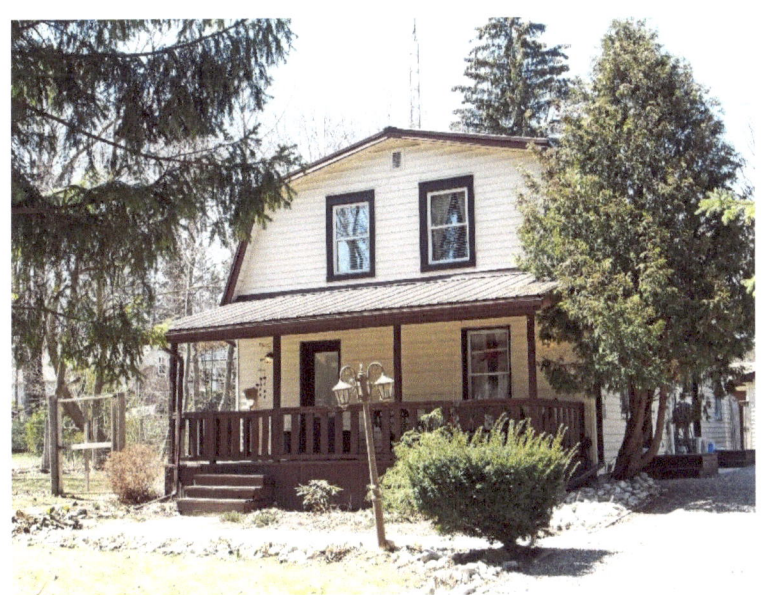

Mill Street – Neo-Colonial – gambrel roof

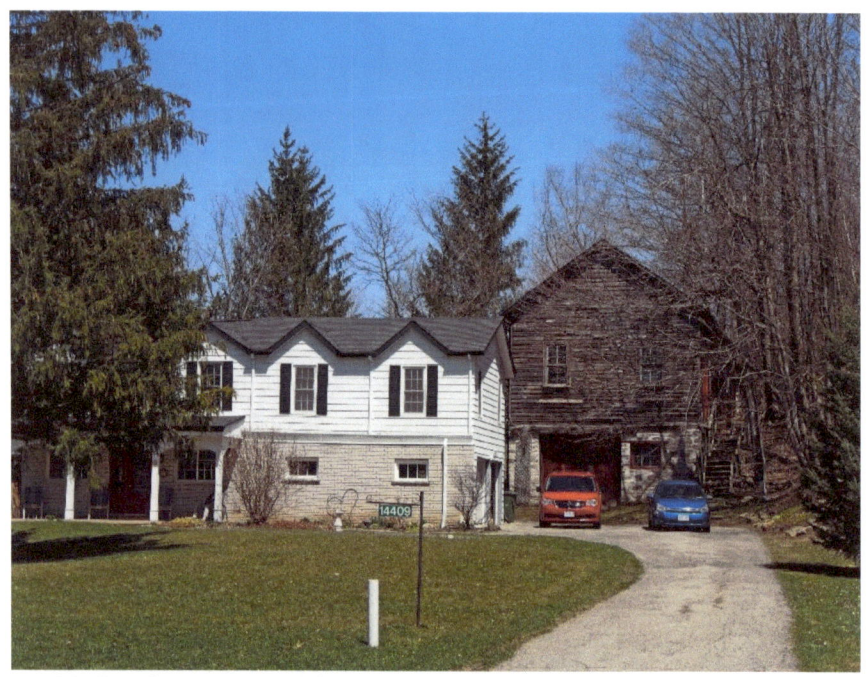

14409 Creditview Road - Beaver Hall - circa 1884 - This 1½ storey timber frame building was built by store owner John Harris, who rented it out to the community for political meetings, concerts and dances until the mid-1930s. Built into the hillside, it has a substantial stone foundation with an 1884 date-stone in the front wall. The main floor is supported with large squared timber beams visible in the unfinished basement ceiling. About 1900, a cement tile business operated from the back of the hall.

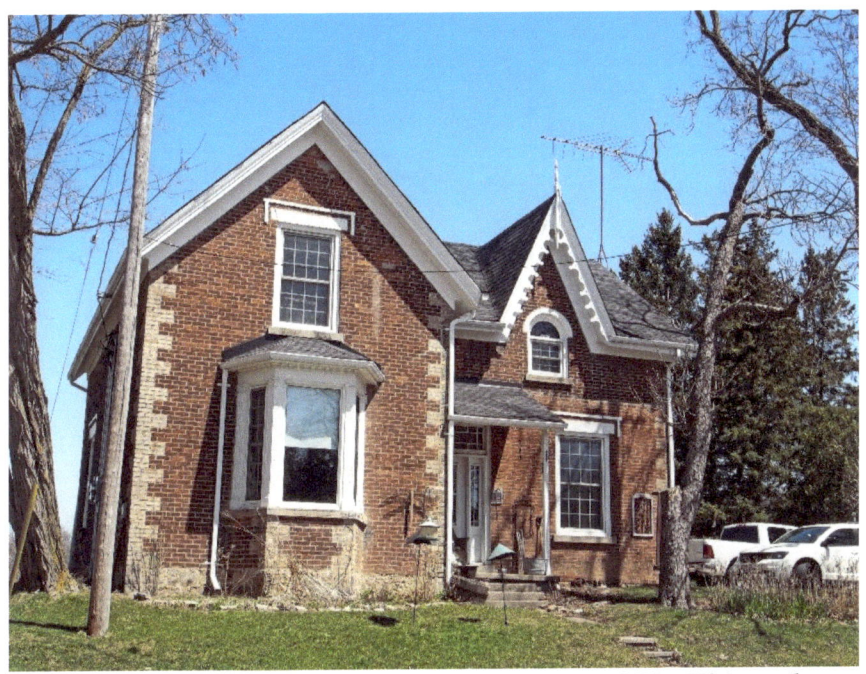

14299 Creditview Road - The Manse - circa 1870 - This red brick Victorian Gothic style house, with yellow brick quoins, was built around 1870. It predates the adjacent church by over 30 years. It later became the United Church manse.

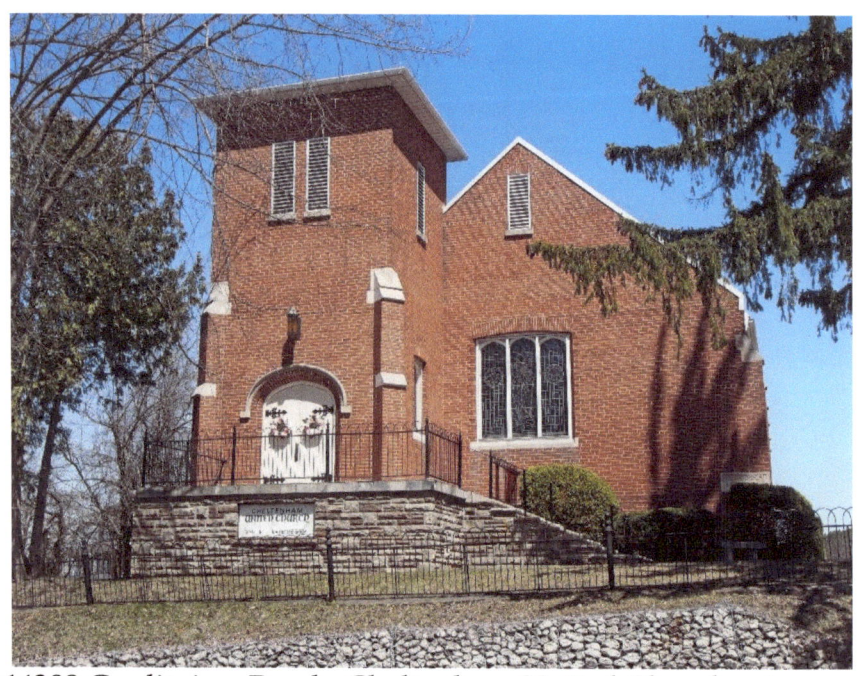

14309 Creditview Road - Cheltenham United Church - circa 1907 - Originally built for a Presbyterian congregation, this church became Cheltenham United Church following church union in 1925. There is a date stone on the south corner of the building.

Terra Cotta

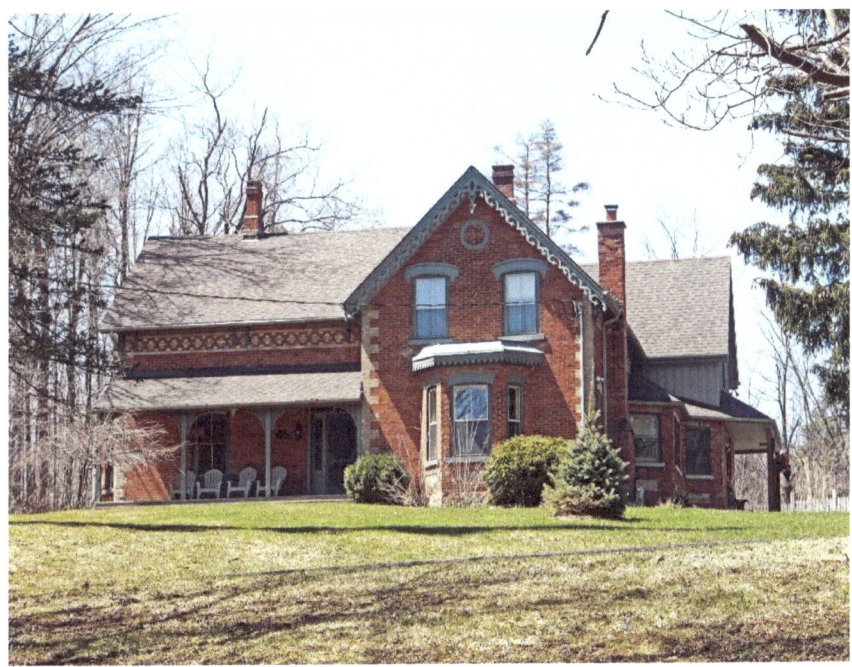

260 King Street - Mill Owner's House - Early 1860s - This large
1½ storey Victorian brick home was built for mill owner
Simon Plewes possibly for his 1863 marriage to Janet Smith.
With a river view, it overlooked his grist and saw mills. The
red bricks were likely locally made from the abundant nearby
clay and are contrasted with yellow brick quoins and
decorative patterning. Simon and Janet had six children.

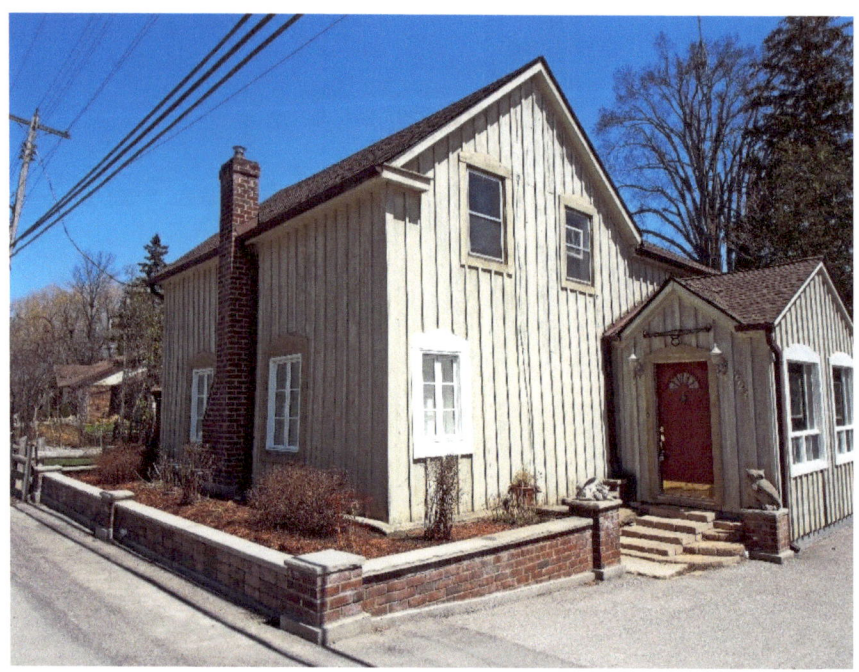

227 King Street - Hotel/Inn - mid 1860s - This simple Neo-Classical style building is Terra Cotta's last standing hotel, originally owned by Thomas and Ann McPherson. It ceased being an Inn in 1900 when blacksmith Robert Gibson converted it to residential use. It was purchased in 1908 by another blacksmith, William G. Marshall. Alterations and additions have obscured the Inn's original centre entrance.

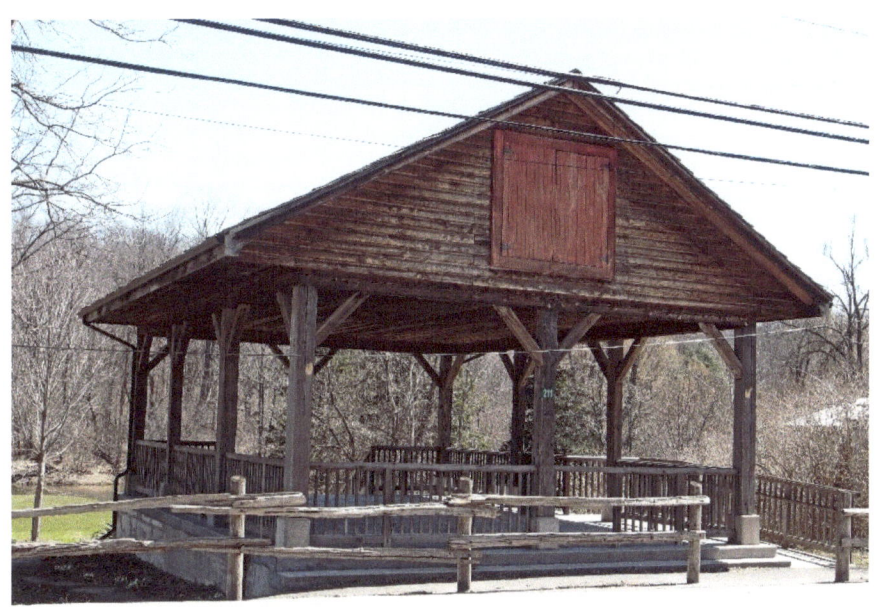

211 King Street - The Forge Park Picnic Shelter - This picnic shelter is on the site of a blacksmith shop first owned by John Leslie in the 1870s. The smithy eventually became a dwelling called 'The Forge' whose doors have been incorporated into the picnic shelter's upper storey.

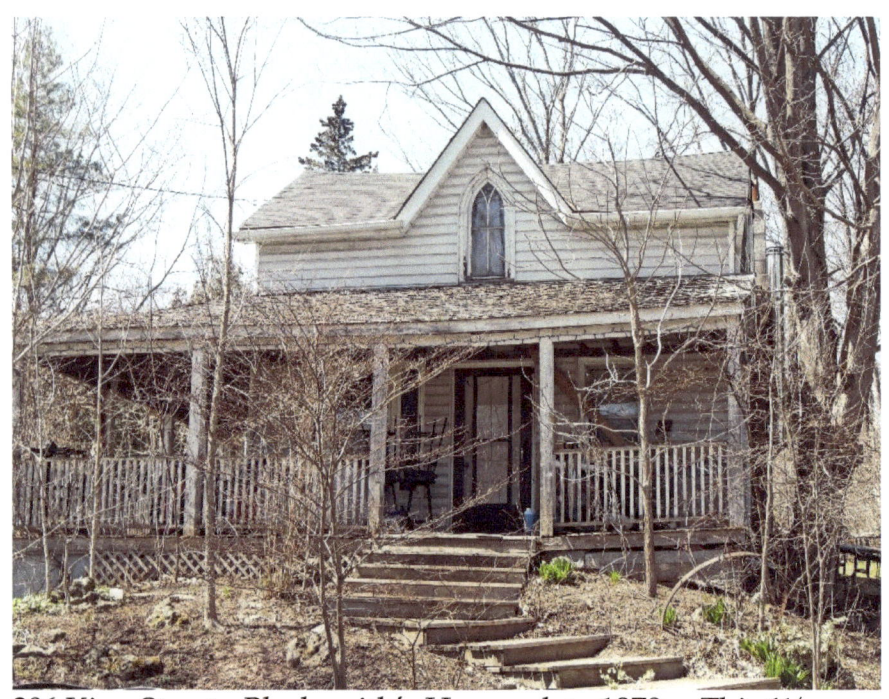

206 King Street - Blacksmith's House - late 1870s - This 1½ storey frame Ontario Cottage was likely built by William Wright and features a centre gable Gothic window, centre entry and full front veranda. In 1881, it was sold to the first of several blacksmiths starting with James Carroll, then Robert Gibson in 1900, followed by William G. Marshall in 1908. Gibson and Marshall likely used this house for worker accommodation or for rental.

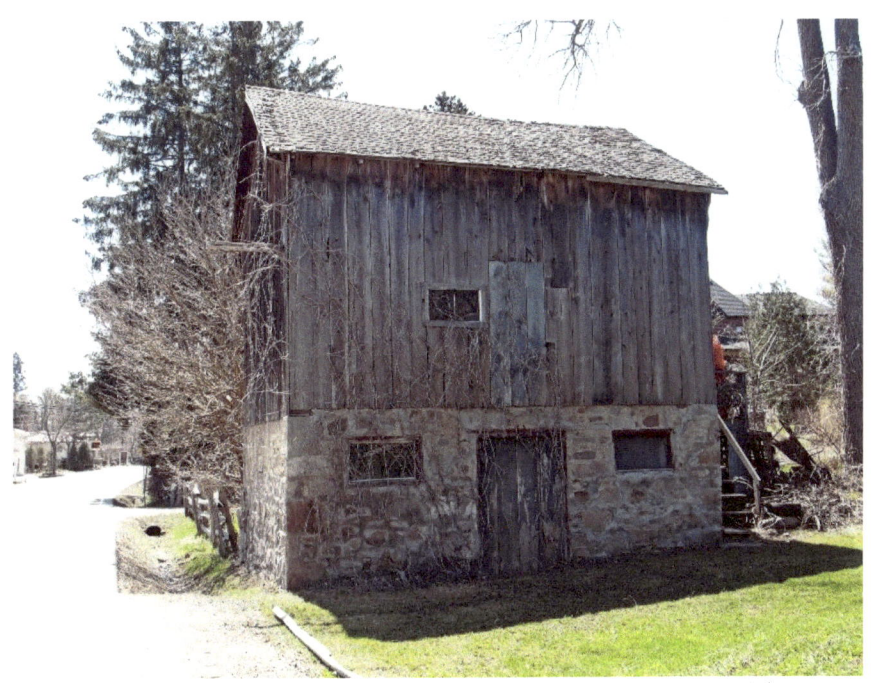

206 King Street - Carriage Works outbuilding - 1900 - This small building with its original rubble stone foundation, vertical plank walls and sign holder was built by blacksmith Robert Gibson. It was part of a carriage works built by Gibson on this site and which included a woodworking shop and paint shop. The enterprise was sold to another blacksmith, William G. Marshall, in 1908 and flourished until motor cars impacted the need both for blacksmiths and for carriages.

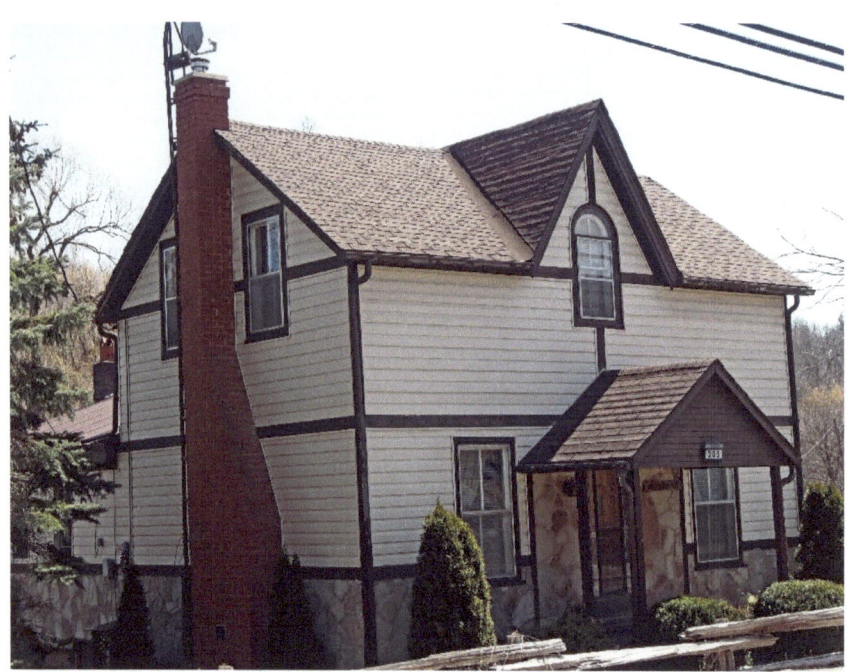

205 King Street - Victorian Gothic Cottage - late 1870s-1880s -
This 1½ storey frame Ontario Cottage was likely built by
Daniel Townsend.   Ownership changed frequently in the
earliest years until Annie Taylor and veteran Toronto
policeman, Charles Taylor, retired here in 1942.

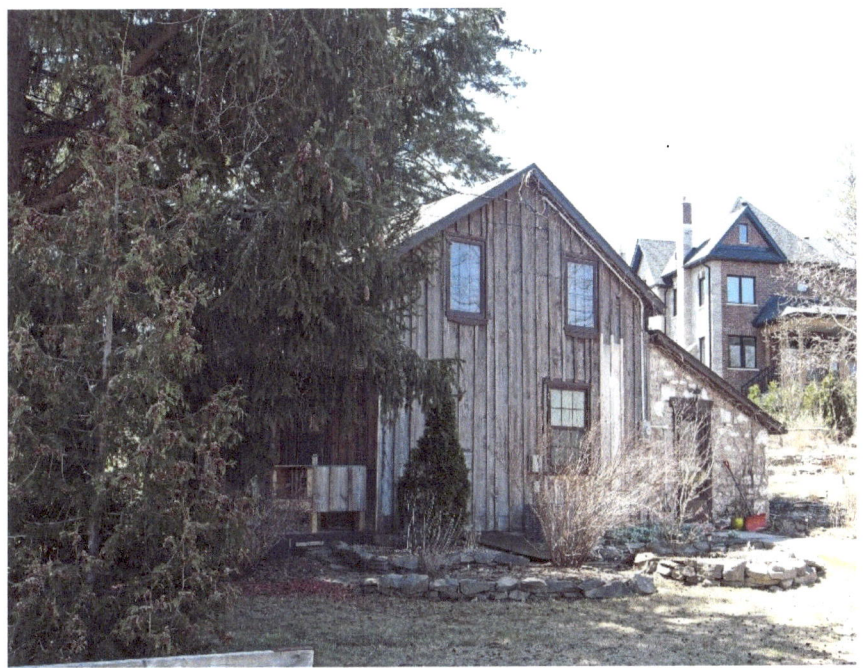

196 King Street - William McPherson House - late 1870s - Built by William McPherson, this 1½ storey frame Ontario Cottage was originally clad with stucco. The verandah and centre gable Gothic window are obscured by massive trees, but a stone extension is visible.

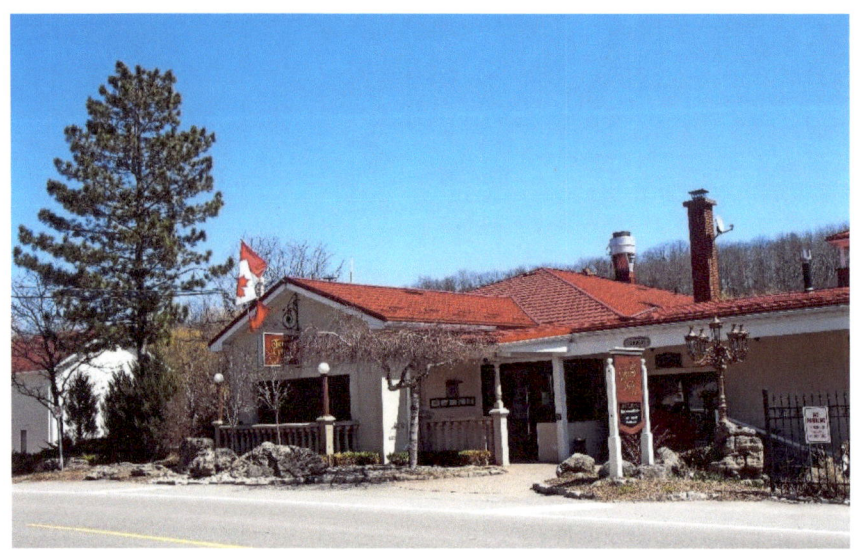

175 King Street - Terra Cotta Inn - late 1880s - The original buildings on this site, dating from the late 1800s, included a general store, barber shop and ice cream parlour. They were purchased in 1949 by Harry and Betty Farrar who converted them to an inn. With two upper floor guest rooms, the inn became locally famous for English style dinners, especially in summer and fall. The inn became a restaurant in 1994.

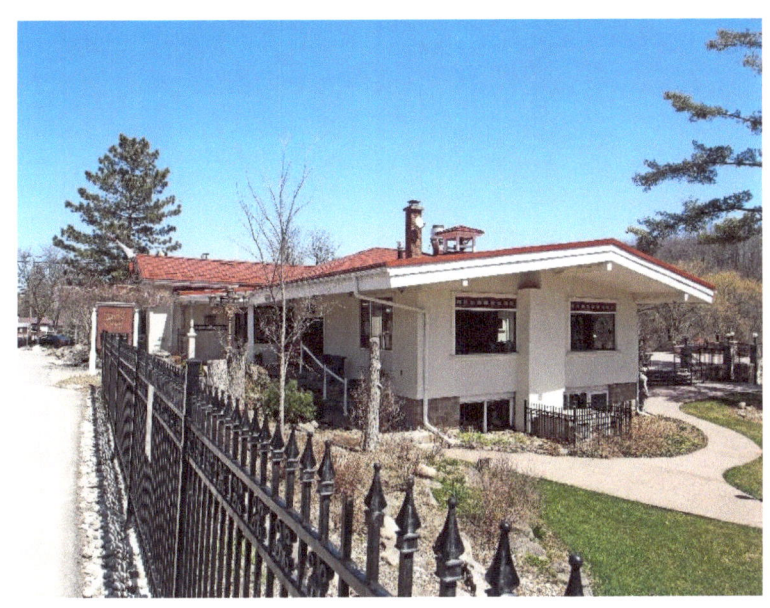

175 King Street

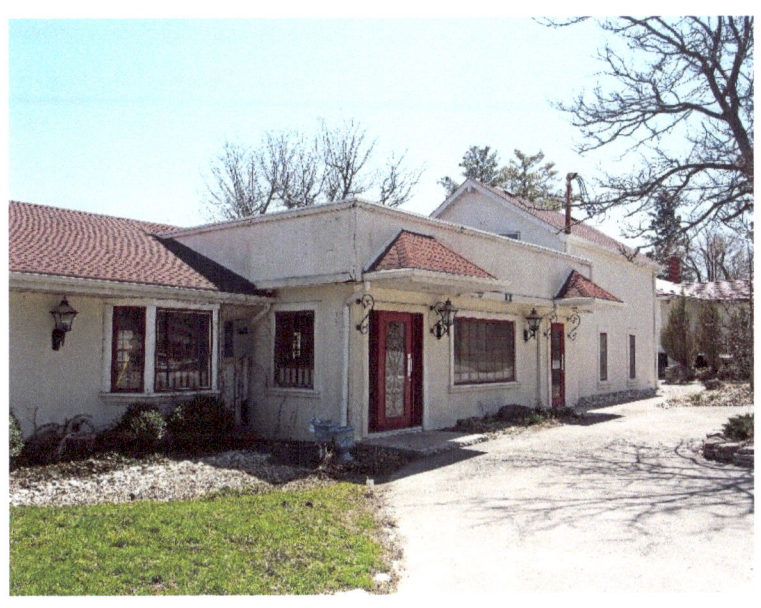

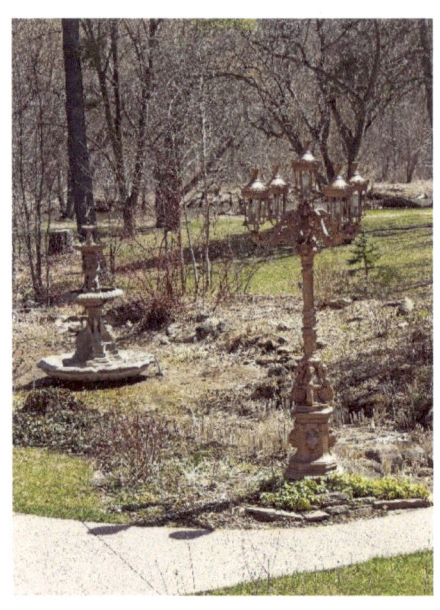

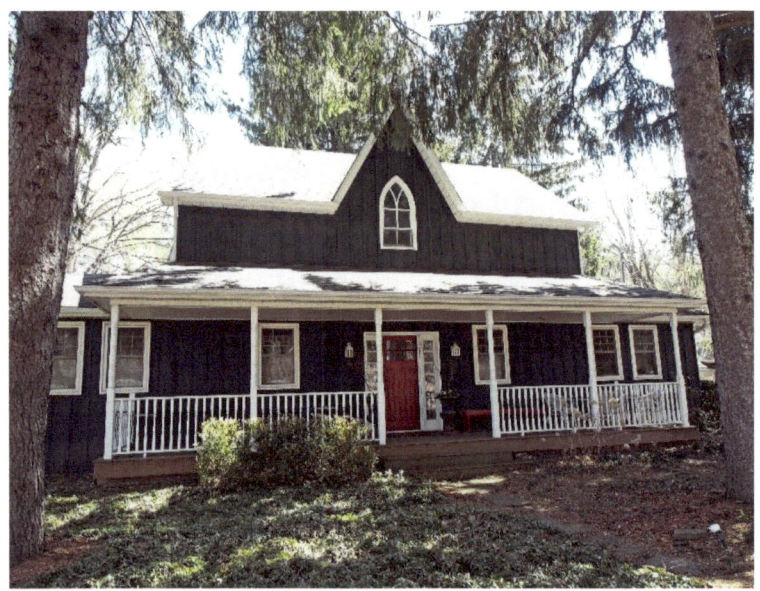

King Street - Gothic Ontario Cottage

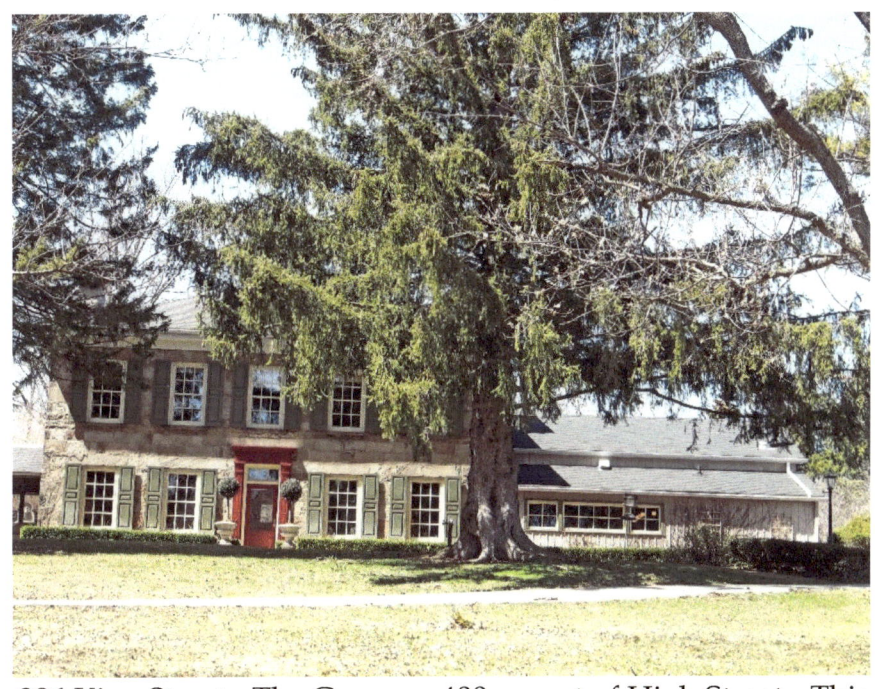

396 King Street - The Grange - 400 m east of High Street - This building has evolved from John McComb's 1840s squared timber cottage. In 1867 George Campbell and his brother William modified it into a two-family stone dwelling. It was inherited by George Campbell's daughters in 1887 and later sold to Edward and Janet Little in whose hands it evolved into this elegant residence.

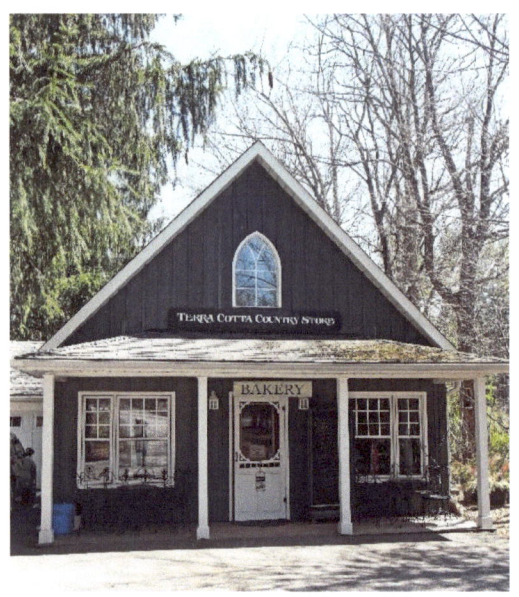

119 King Street - Terra Cotta Country Store

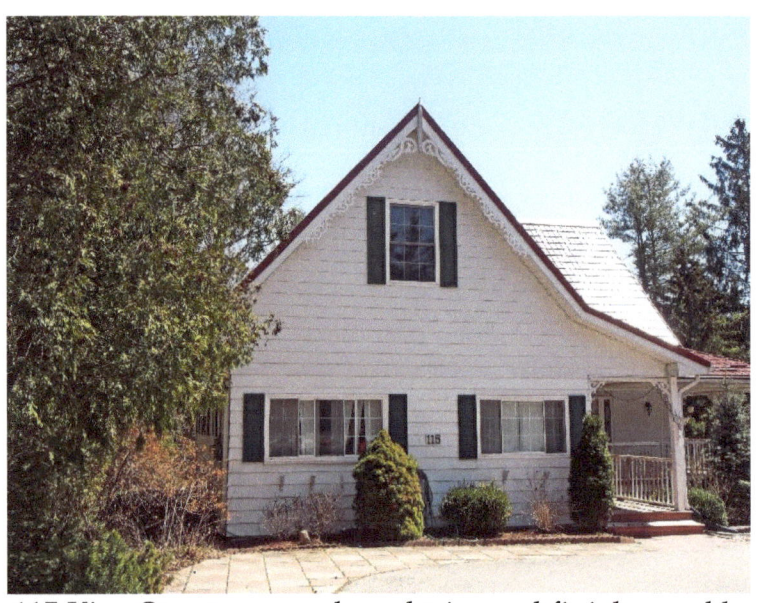

115 King Street – verge board trim and finial on gable

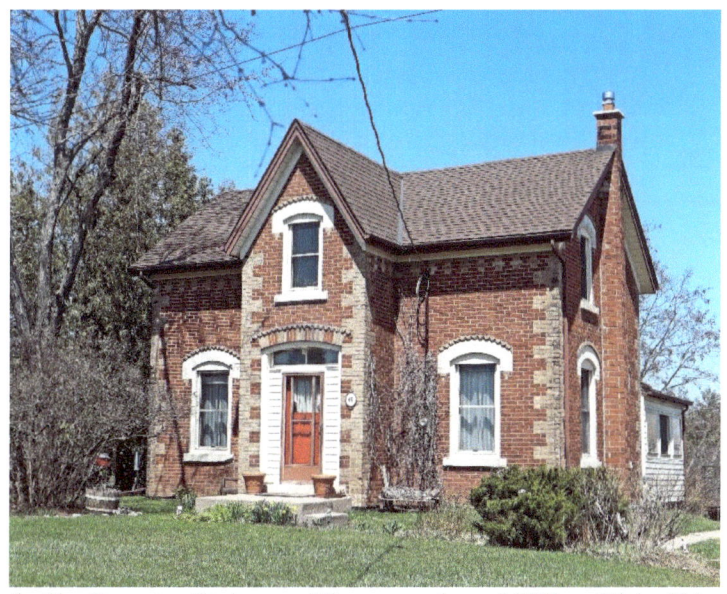

49 Isabella Street - Stringer House - circa 1870s - This 1½ storey Victorian Gothic house was originally a frame cottage later veneered in the red and yellow brick produced locally by Terra Cotta Pressed Brick. The projecting front bay has yellow brick detailing.

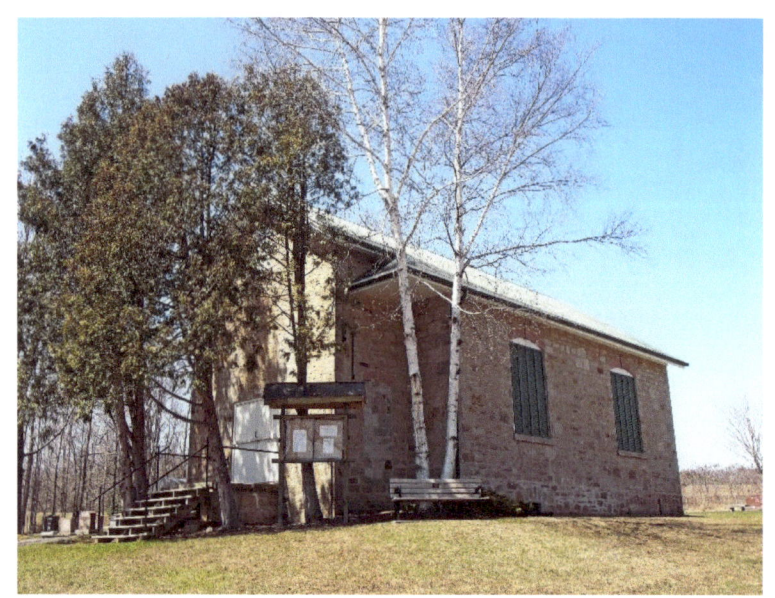

1942 Boston Mills Road – Boston Mills Cemetery since 1823

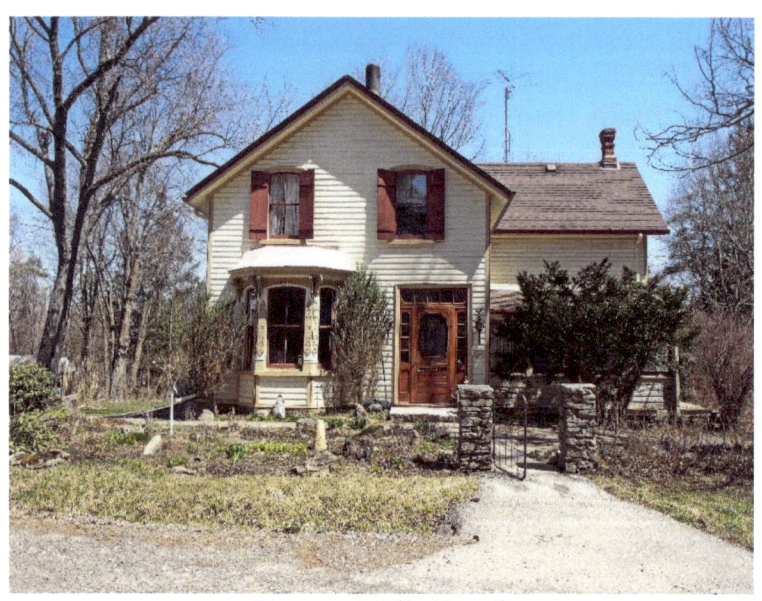

Boston Mills Road

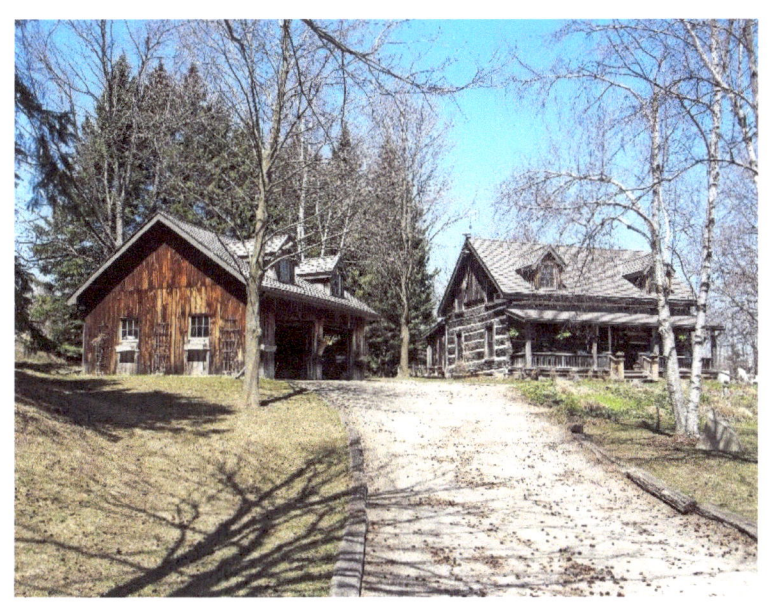

Boston Mills Road – log cabin

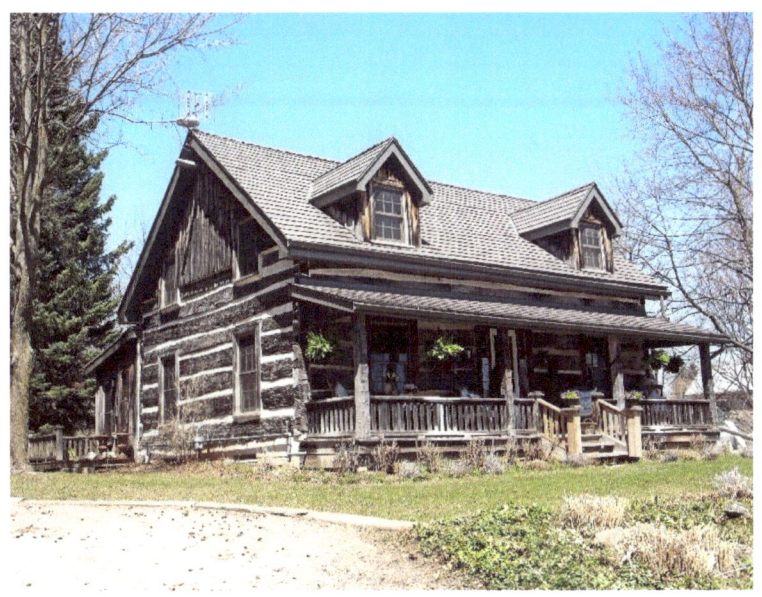

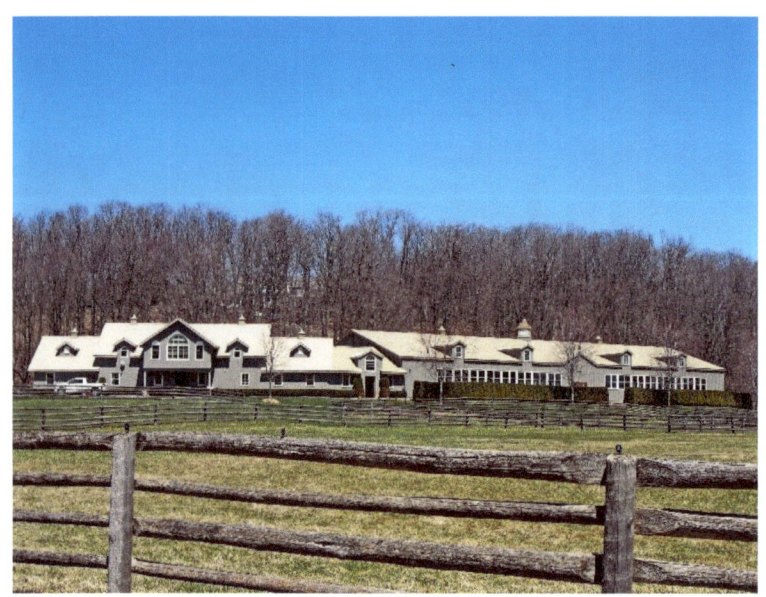

Creditview Road

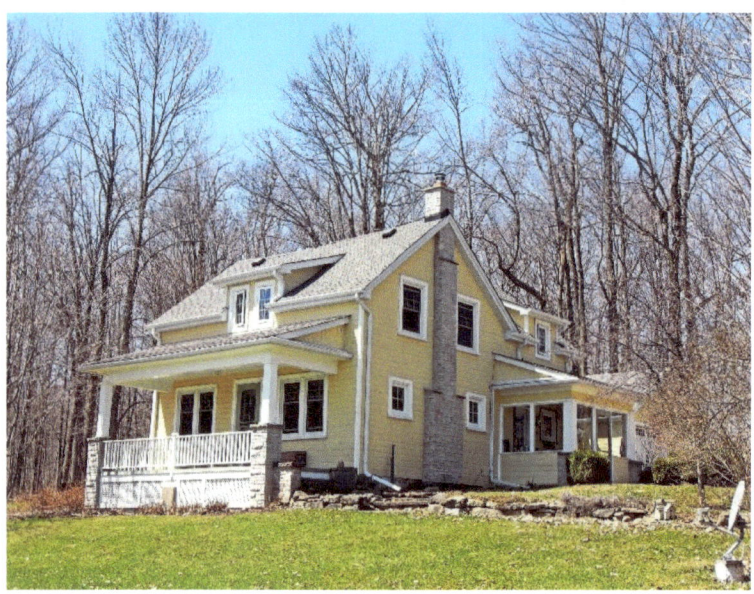

Creditview Road

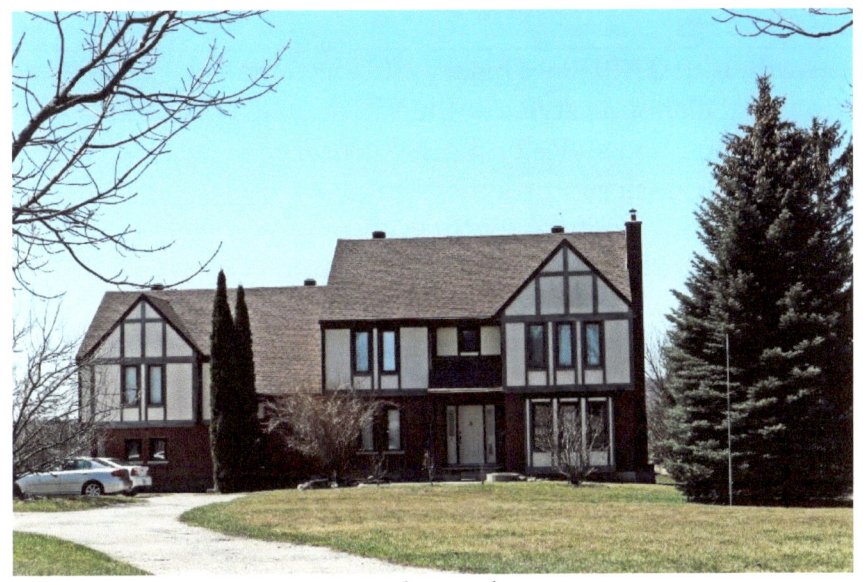

Tudor style

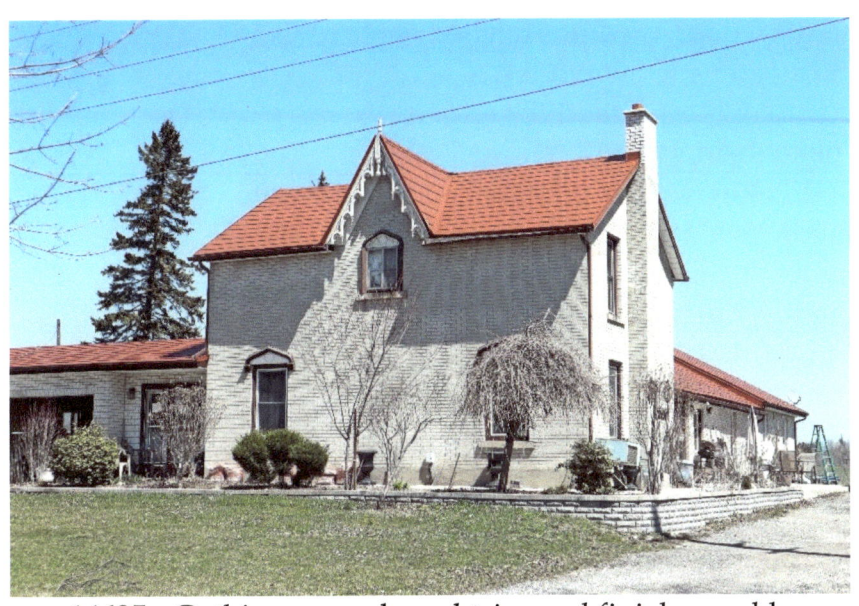

14635 - Gothic – verge board trim and finial on gable

Edwardian, 1900-1930 – This style bridges the ornate and elaborate styles of the Victorian era and the simplified styles of the 20th century. Edwardian Classicism provided simple, balanced facades, simple rooflines, dormer windows, large front porches, and smooth brick surfaces. Voussoirs and keystones are used sparingly and are understated. Finials and cresting are absent. Cornice brackets and braces are block-like and openings have flat arches or plain stone lintels. Example: 14387 Creditview Road, Cheltenham, Page 13	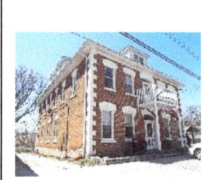
Georgian, before 1860 – This style began with the British King Georges in the 18th century. These buildings have balanced facades around a central door, medium-pitched gable roofs, and small paned windows. Example: 14396 Creditview Road, Cheltenham, Page 12	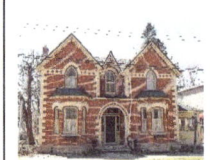
Gothic Revival, 1830-1890 – These decorative buildings have sharply-pitched gables with highly detailed verge boards, pointed-arch window openings, and dichromatic brickwork. It is a common style in Ontario. Example: 14376 Creditview Road, Cheltenham, Page 5	

The **Farmhouse** is a country home style that highlights the simplicity of rural living. Comfort and function are the major themes that are associated with the style. The roof frequently flares out to cover the porch. The large porches were designed to help cool the interior of the home and also provide a shady spot for guests to gather and enjoy the outdoors. The architecture of a country home is minimally ornamental but very efficient with functional shutters, decorative porch railing, and dormer windows that increase interior light and living space. The exterior is typically faced with horizontal siding. Farmhouse floor plans are usually square or symmetrically shaped, sometimes with side wings. The interior has a large country kitchen and a cluster of bedrooms on the upper level. Farmhouses contain at least one fireplace and large family gathering areas designed for relaxation. The country home is casual, functional and comfortable. Well-crafted and sturdy, farmhouses are generally built to last and withstand for ages.
Example: 14529 Creditview Road, Cheltenham, Page 8

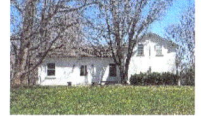

A **log cabin**, built from logs, was usually one-or 1½-storeys constructed with round rather than hewn, or hand-worked, logs, and erected quickly for frontier shelter. Log cabins were built from logs laid horizontally and interlocked on the ends with notches. The cabin was situated to provide sunlight and drainage so the pioneers could cope better with the rigors of frontier life. The pioneers chose old-growth trees that were straight and had few knots and did not need to be hewn to fit well together. Careful notching minimized the size of the gap between the logs and reduced the amount of chinking with sticks and rocks or daubing with mud to fill the gap. The length of one log was the length of one wall.

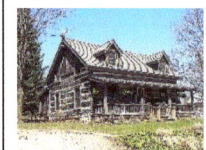

Example: Boston Mills Road, Page 41

Neo-Classical, 1810-1850 – This style was a direct result of the War of 1812. Many Upper Canadians returning from the war with the United States were second or third generation Loyalists who had inherited land and means from their forefathers. Once the conflict had passed, they had the money and the time to expand their holdings and indulge their architectural whims. Both residential and commercial buildings were constructed on the traditional Georgian plan, but they had a new gaiety and light-heartedness. Detailing became more refined, delicate, and elegant. Example: 227 King Street, Terra Cotta, Page 28	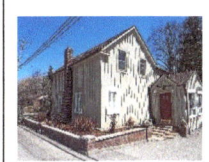
Neo-colonial (also Colonial Revival, Georgian Revival or Neo-Georgian) architecture seeks to revive elements of architectural style of American colonial architecture of the period around the Revolutionary War which drew strongly from Georgian architecture of Great Britain. Architecture from the 18th and early 19th centuries in Ontario includes a wide assortment of detailing and ornament applied to a design centered around the fireplace and the source of water. Structures are typically two stories, have a symmetrical front facade with elaborate front doorways, often with decorative crown pediments, fanlights, and sidelights, symmetrical windows flanking the front entrance, often in pairs or threes, and columned porches. Example: Mill Street, Cheltenham, Page 23	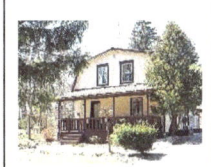

Ontario Cottage - one or one-and-a-half story buildings with a cottage or hip roof. The cottage roof is an equal hip roof where each hip extends to a point in the center of the roof. The hip roof has a long hip in the center. The Ontario Cottage is the vernacular design of the Regency Cottage which generally has a more ornate doorway and a partial or full verandah surrounding it. The roof can have a dormer, a belvedere, and generally two chimneys. Example: 206 King Street, Terra Cotta, Page 30	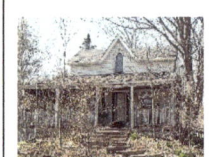
Tudor Revival – exposed timbers with stucco infill, multi-paned windows. Example: Page 43	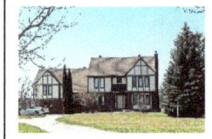
Victorian - In Ontario, a Victorian style building can be seen as any building built between 1840 and 1900 that doesn't fit into any of the other categories. It encompasses a large group of buildings constructed in brick, stone, and timber, using an eclectic mixture of Classical and Gothic motifs. Example: 260 King Street, Terra Cotta, Page 27	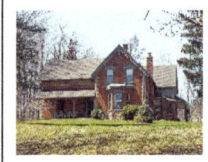

Other Books by Barbara Raue

Coins of Gold
Arrows, Indians and Love
The Life and Times of Barbara
The Cromwell Family Book
Laura Secord Discovered
Daddy Where Are You?

Montana Series
Book 1: Montana Dream
Book 2: Life on the Montana Frontier
Book 3: Montana to Boston and Back
Book 4: Montana Sons Go to War
Book 5: Montana Sons Return from War